hanson

the boys from nowhere

Created by Pop Culture, published by OZone Books, a division of Bobcat Books, distributed by Book
Sales Ltd., Newmarket Road, Bury St. Edmunds, Suffolk IP33 3YB.

Copyright © 1997 OZone Books

Order No: OZ100056
ISBN 1 90182703 8

Picture credits: All Action, Redferns, Retna Pictures Limited, Star File Photo Agency Limited.
Cover Picture: Retna Pictures Limited

Design by:

hanson

the boys from nowhere

by Velimir Pavle Ilic

CLARKE ISAAC HANSON

Age: 16
D.O.B: 17th November 1980
Birthplace: Tulsa, Oklahoma
Height: 5ft 10ins
Weight: 10st 5lbs

Ike's jobs in the band are guitarist and backing singer. You might like to know that he also got to demonstrate the full power of his lungs on the track 'Minute Without You', as he sings lead vocals.

STAR SIGN: SCORPIO

As a Scorpian Ike has a majestic presence, oozing charm and charisma. Being a natural leader (his nickname is 'Leader') he manages to keep his brothers in line, protecting them and laying down the law when necessary. Ike is the intelligent member of the group, who is good at working out problems. Look out though, just as Ike may make you feel relaxed in his sensitive company, he can lash out with that stinger and show you his hot temper.

IS HE A ROMANTIC?

Ike claims that he is a romantic. Let's see! - As a Scorpian he can be passionate and sensual, but again that sting can come out when he shows you his jealous and possessive sides. Taureans, Pisceans, and Liberians he's the guy for you. Arieans, Geminis, Leos and Aquarians beware!
Isaac is currently single, and says that the touring makes dating impossible. Still, he is on the look!
Zac and Taylor say Ike's the romantic one in the band.

OTHER FACTS:

• Ike's fave food is a good steak, and he is partial to a bit of Italian such as lasagne and spaghetti.
• Ike's bad habit is biting his fingernails
• His favourite TV shows are 'Seinfeld' and 'Single Guy'
• Ike has passed his driving test so he can now drive the vans when the band are on tour.
• Isaac is still waiting for his first proper kiss!
• Ike is currently writing a science fiction novel.

HANSON FACTS!

STAR SIGN: PISCES

Taylor is creative and enjoys nothing more than having the freedom to express himself. Music brings him peace and contentment.

Taylor also possesses a great imagination and can be a bit of a dreamer. Still, he will be able to stick with reality long enough to achieve great things. As a Piscean, Taylor is loving, caring and sensitive. But look out because he may need a good shoulder to cry on occasionally, being slightly over emotional. Look out for Taylor in his melodramatic stage! However, he is humorous and always good company.

IS HE A ROMANTIC?

Taylor will need to be told he is loved and adored often and will hate rejection. However, he could slip out of a relationship himself, being a bit of a drifter. He will pay you lots of attention though when in a relationship. Ideal for Liberians and Leos. Taylor is currently single, but loves to spend times between shows signing autographs for girls.

Ike and Zac say that Tay is a perfectionist.

OTHER FACTS:

• Taylor's nickname is Blondie (wonder why?)

• His fave TV shows are 'Friends', 'Frasier', and 'Seinfeld'.

• Taylor's favourite food is burgers and fries.

• His habit is to tap away at any surface in front of him. Forever the keyboard player!

• Taylor is quite sporty. He enjoys rollerblading and go-karting.

JORDAN TAYLOR HANSON

Age: 14
D.O.B: 14th March 1983
Birthplace: Tulsa, Oklahoma
Height: 5ft 7ins
Weight: 8st 13lbs

Taylor's job in the band is as main vocalist. He also plays the keyboard and does percussion.

ZACHARY WALKER HANSON

Age: 11
D.O.B: 22nd October 1985
Birthplace: Arlington, Virginia
Height: 5ft
Weight: 6st 1lbs

Zac's job in the band is as drummer and he does some backing singing. Zachary gets to show off his great voice to the max on the tracks 'Lucy' and 'Man From Milwaukee' (penned by Zac himself).

STAR SIGN: LIBRA

Zac is a typical Libra and enjoys lots and lots of attention. He is also very artistic, musical and enjoys computers, clothes, and dancing. Zac is a very good communicator; he is honest and will charm your socks off. However, you best keep your eyes open for Zac has his bad points. He can be sulky, a little overpowering and just about as vain as they come. Don't boss him about, he will not like it. Give him lots of reassurance though.

IS HE A ROMANTIC?

Although Zac will be very loving, he will be the dependent one. You will have to make the moves to get him to be a bit more independent. Aries, go for it! Capricorns, Cancerians, Pisceans and Taureans take care!

Zac does not have a girlfriend right now, but he loves it when girls scream for the band.

Taylor and Isaac say Zac has a split personality. Sometimes quiet...then crazy!

OTHER FACTS

• Zac's nickname is Animal (just look at him on those drums).
• His fave TV show is the Animaniacs.
• Zac will eat just about anything!
• Zac has a habit of being a little bit too physical.
• Zac is into Nintendo and Sega.

ALL ABOUT HANSON

*The ideas for the 'MMMBop' video came from the boys themselves. Wild imaginations, eh!

*The Hanson clan extends a lot further than the talented trio. Walker and Diana Hanson are also the proud parents of daughters Jessie (8), Avie (6), and youngest son Mac (3).

*The boys started performing together 5 years ago.

*Ike, Taylor, and Zac write their own material, and yes they really can play those instruments.

*Hanson's influences include the likes of Chuck Berry, Aretha Franklin, and the Supremes. (Just like Jacko!)

*The boys enjoy sitting in their treehouse at home in Tulsa. They built it themselves.

*Hanson will be touring Australia and the Far East later this year.

*Hanson used to dress alike. They all wore black leather jackets in their early shows. Now they have decided that was too corny.

*Before Mercury signed them the boys were turned down by 12 labels.

*'Middle Of Nowhere' is actually Hanson's third album. 'Boomerang' and 'MMMBop' came before. Sound familiar?

*The Internet is crammed with both pro and anti -Hanson websites. So log on.

*'MMMBop' the boys tell us is about friendships, and the many different relationships you can have in life. (No doubt there will be lots more to come for the lads).

*You will soon be able to cuddle up to Hanson every night. Hanson dolls are coming soon!

*Hanson have performed about 300 shows in their short career.

*One of Zac's hobbies is to invent comic books.

Look out for more Hanson Facts!

introduction

Records on the radio. Thousands of them. Some of them get stuck in your head for hours, others do not. It is 1997, and as April rolls headlong into May, Hanson's 'MMMBop' definitely falls into the former category. You have undoubtedly found yourself humming it, perhaps not even realising that you are doing so. Everyone, unless they have been on Mars for the past few months, knows who these boys are. You can not fail to have missed those cherubic, pouting grins beaming out at you every which way you turn. Love 'em or hate 'em, Hanson have arrived. 'MMMBop' is a catchy, unashamedly sugary tune made for the summer, and it comes swathed in a breezy harmony that is hard to resist. We do not yet know whether it is the beginning of a long, commercially successful career, but considering it is most people's first taste of the band, it seems to have hit all the right spots. The single's success in the USA, the UK and Europe has maximised their profile to the full from day one. With the release of their third album, 'Middle Of Nowhere', this has been cemented even more into the subconscious of the music-buying public, and even at this early stage in their careers, they are beginning to cause controversy and debate. The Internet is full of both pro- and anti-Hanson web sites, (there are over two hundred to date), which just shows the amount of interest they have created. It raises a fascinatingly moot point; if one observes the number of spelling mistakes contained within the pro-Hanson communication as opposed to the anti-Hanson stuff, it would seem that the anti-Hanson brigade are significantly more literate. Sure, the backbiters tend to be adolescents, and the band may be designed to appeal mainly to the younger teen market, but it would be foolish to dismiss them as one-hit wonders. They are actually gifted songwriters, which is something that cannot easily be said of the entire boy-pop genre. The infiltration of young bands into the system is on the increase. With groups like grunge merchants Silverchair, Fiona Apple and rock starlets Radish (who include within their line-up 16-year old Ben Kweller). Also LeAnn Rimes (14 year old country singer, who won the 1997 Grammy award for Best New Artist) and Jonny Lang, a 16-year old blues guitarist with a speaking voice almost as deep as Barry White's. Britain's own Symposium are at the forefront, fighting (with varying degrees of success) for recognition. Hanson, it would be fair to say, are in good company.

the boys from nowhere

*One of Hanson's first big gigs was at the Blue Rose Café in Tulsa. Unfortunately they had to play in the parking lot because none of them were old enough to enter the bar.

From Nowhere

The age of the wunderkind is upon us yet again - as a breed they are set apart, yet their age is also the unique feature that casts them into the fluctuating, fickle glare of the media spotlight. Radio One's Steve Lamacq has already championed Radish's cause, attaching a tag of instant credibility to anything they do. Record labels may currently be looking to sign younger groups, with one eye on potential long-term staying power and the other on what should hopefully be ensuing profits, but junior bands in the current climate are generally shrewder and less likely to be exploited. The record companies have wisely tapped into this narrow vein of logic along the way. They have come to appreciate that raw adolescent attitudes are characteristics that have been taken for granted and trodden on in the past, but which now actually form the vital crux of the whole teeny-bop wrangle. The psyche of youth, generally untainted by cynicism, has the advantage of 'total' enthusiasm, and certainly in the case of Hanson we have a teenage trio who are yet to discover the meaning of the phrase 'angst-ridden'. Their pop formula is so disconcerting, so canny, and so able. Whichever way you look at it, Hanson are talented youngsters, with songs in their fledgling repertoire that will appeal to a large cross-section of people (as much as they will irritate others).

Born and raised mainly in the drilling town of Tulsa, Oklahoma, they have seemingly appeared from nowhere, but there is a story to tell. The three brothers (Clarke Isaac Hanson (Ike), Jordan Taylor Hanson (Tay), and Zachary Walker Hanson (Zac)) have been into music from an early age. Indeed their burgeoning career is made all the more remarkable by the fact that they are still teenagers, although once you take their musical history into consideration you sense that sooner or later it was always going to end up this way. The tale of Isaac, 16 (born 17th November, 1980), Taylor, 14 (born 14th March, 1983) and Zachary, 11 (born 22nd October, 1985) begins in earnest years ago, when their parents (Walker and Diana) taught them to sing a harmonious "Amen" at the end of the dinner table blessing. In fact one of Diana's favourite songwriters is the prolific Billy Joel, and his song 'For The Longest Time' was one of the first complete tunes the Hanson brothers sang along to. It was not long before the boys could concoct their own pitch-perfect harmonies, which were based around their lengthy exposure to traditional 1950s and 1960s rock and soul, and the Christian songs that had underpinned their upbringing. Beginning with two-part harmonies, they moved up to three-part and then gradually added backing tapes and instruments.

To Somewhere

They would be roped in for family reunions and company parties, taking the opportunity to perform their a cappella harmonies anywhere they could. Walker recalls that during this period, *"we wrote a lot of songs about frogs and ants...(!)"*. The next logical step was to begin writing songs of a more mature and realistic frame (which they entered into with hefty aplomb), and it was Isaac who wrote his first song at the age of 8, with Taylor joining in on harmony soon afterwards. Both Walker and Diana had a history of musical involvement going right back to their high school days (they travelled regularly to perform with a gospel group, and would constantly be walking around singing various classics and improvising). Walker and Diana were married at the relatively young age of 19 (during their first year at the University of Oklahoma), and both adored music. With Walker's own aptitude on piano and guitar, combined with Diana's experience as a one-time professional singer, it was inevitable that the boys would follow suit, although the roots of their interest in music stem from even richer sources. Walker Hanson's job as an international financier for an oil company meant frequent relocation (Venezuela, Trinidad, Ecuador), and it was during this time that his young sons became captivated with the Time-Life compilation records (spanning the years 1957-1969) that constituted part of his and Diana's record collection. Check out the list of influences: Chuck Berry, Bobby Darin, Johnnie Taylor, Aretha Franklin, Little Richard, Elvis Presley, The Supremes, and later acts such as The Beach Boys, Otis Redding, The Monkees, Sly Stone and The Jackson Five. Quite a selection!

Even in those earlier days, Hanson-mania was in evidence. The boys had pestered their parents into allowing them to go and perform at the Tulsa Mayfest (a kind of arts festival) in 1992, which is where they made their live debut singing *a cappella* medleys of 1950s cover versions, adorned in leather jackets and sunglasses. Following this, they performed locally at various festivals and parties, and even began to play at school assemblies in front of screaming, pre-teen schoolgirls. They had begun to get quite a following, which encouraged their parents to pay for the pressing of a couple of thousand albums. They sold these at their shows and in local record stores. Money was never a real problem with the Hanson's - Walker's high-income occupation meant that he could comfortably support the boys' euphonious intentions.

Having had extensive classical piano training, the brothers also began to master other instruments, which eventually resulted in the abandonment of their vocals-only stance to become more of an 'electric' band. Ike bought a second-hand guitar, Taylor borrowed a keyboard from a friend, and Zac channelled his natural energy into flailing around on a Ludwig drum-kit, which his father had managed to fish out from the attic. Every spare moment had to be utilised. Dishes remained unwashed as the boys took the opportunity to practice their singing - their parents would return from a shopping trip to find the kitchen in the same state in which they had left it two hours before! Neither was it unusual for the boys to practice in the bathroom, where they would use available resources to their advantage. The ceramic tiling on the floor and in the shower applied the most excellent echo vibrato effect to their vocals! The photograph on the inner sleeve of 'Middle Of Nowhere' features the boys holding their instruments in a black bathroom. It might be a posed shot, but it obviously is not as unrealistic as it may seem. Nevertheless, music was not the only priority.

Education was an important issue in the lives of the young Hansons, to the extent that their parents felt they would benefit more from home schooling than from a normal classroom environment. Exams were sat at the dining table and posted to the local authority for marking, but the trio do not feel as if they have missed out on anything by not attending school. It did not interfere with their music - once the homework had been completed, they would rush into the living room to play their instruments. Even now, they take a tutor with them on their travels. The arrangements were perfect, if only because the constraints of Walker's occupation meant that they were forced to move around South America for a while. At times, the experience of different cultures has been a bonus, as Zac explained in a recent chat with Smash Hits magazine, whilst in London:

"We're experiencing new people and new cultures. Things like the London Dungeons and the Tower Of London History Ride - how many U.S. history teachers would die to be able to send their class to London?"

*The boys have lived in places such as Venezuela, Trinidad, and Ecuador.

By travelling all over the world, Hanson claim they can learn much more than they ever could from having their noses stuck in a book. Their parents have planned this system to perfection from the start, and it seems to have worked like a charm, even early on, when the three older brothers were beginning to experience a heavy gigging schedule. As well as schooling the children at home, including the other three Hanson siblings: sisters, Jessica (8), Avery (6), and brother Mackenzie (3), Diana also found the time to book venues for the three senior Hansons. Not to be left out, Walker would help with unloading their equipment before each show. The family travelled almost anywhere for the chance to play live - New Orleans, Chicago, Los Angeles and Kansas City. The list just goes on and on. In fact, since 1992, Hanson have performed in public hundreds of times, and have written more than two hundred songs. The irony is that when they played the Blue Rose Café (a hip and happening Tulsa bar owned by a friend of theirs), they actually had to perform in the parking lot, as they were not old enough to get in! It worked out to their advantage, drawing crowds of appreciative people who had initially just happened to be passing. Satisfying the burger and lemonade orders of the impromptu audience also ensured that the café's profits received a terrific boost, whilst Diana in turn capitalised on the turnout, taking the opportunity to sell CDs and T-shirts to the appreciative throng. The fan base was increasing all the time, along with their higher profile performances - a major plus was their appearance at the NAIA Men's National Basketball Championships, a highlight of the American sporting calendar. Almost without realising it, the group have used their image and their age to their own distinct advantage. Hanson do what they do with scant regard for hype or consequence, but being young and photogenic is surely a huge bonus, and without question, it has been a useful tool in their relatively speedy rise. The switch from page-boy haircuts to long, blond locks and clothes that just erred on the right side of scruffy was a stroke of genius, as this new 'slacker' look would appeal to both the teen and the indie market. It was also around this time that they clipped the group moniker from the Hanson Brothers to the more straightforward Hanson (having originally been called The Hansons!). More than ever, the telephone calls to the Hanson family home were coming thick and fast - these generally consisted of no more than high-pitched screams from excited, pre-pubescent females. Although things were going well, the band were soon to discover that the path to greater glories would not be as easy to conquer.

*Zac loves London. He thinks the Tower of London history Ride is cool.

Time to Grow Up

Christopher Sabec (then a music attorney) was having lunch at a restaurant in Austin, Texas, unaware of his subsequent fate. He was approached by the three brothers Hanson, who had flown out to the South By Southwest Music Convention for unsigned bands in the hope of landing a record deal. Needless to say, they had not been successful and found themselves inside the aforementioned restaurant, wandering through an audience of diners. Sauntering over to Sabec's table, they asked politely if they could sing *a cappella* for him. No one else was paying them any attention, so he agreed to their request for an impromptu performance. Immediately awe-struck, he promptly asked to speak to their parents, and was virtually inaugurated on the spot as the group's manager. Although everything was still looking rosy, Sabec and the boys were to have a tough spell between 1992-1995. They did not waste any time in trying to sell Hanson to the major record companies, but during that three year stretch, twelve labels actually passed on them (including their eventual home, Mercury). There were no signatures to be scribbled on contracts this time around. Sabec remarked that most labels had advised him to *"get away from this act as fast as possible."* Some had even gone as far as to say that Hanson would do no more than ruin and humiliate their manager. Events had taken a bleak (yet temporary) turn for the worse, but they continued to perform and released a series of tapes, which they sold at their gigs.

*Walker and Diana Hanson have quite a musical past. Walker can play piano and guitar and Diana was once a professional singer.

Time to Grow Up

It is now well into 1995, and Hanson release their first independent CD, entitled 'Boomerang'. It is a glossy exercise in pure pop, floating in a spectrum somewhere between Ace of Base and Boyz II Men, and containing a mix of original songs and cover versions. Isaac vividly recalls trying to create interest in the album by sending it out to different labels, but evidently it was difficult for people to see past the 'white guys singing R&B' premise. Track listing is as follows:

01: Boomerang (original Hanson composition)
02: Poison Ivy
03: Lonely Boy
04: Don't Accuse (original Hanson composition)
05: Rain (original Hanson composition, *a cappella*)
06: More Than Anything (original Hanson composition)
07: The Love You Save (Jackson 5 song)
08: Back To The Island
09: More Than Anything reprise (original Hanson composition)

*Hanson used to rehearse in their bathroom; the tiled surfaces added a great effect to the vocals.

Another release was soon on the cards, on the same independent basis as 'Boomerang'. This time the album title was 'MMMBop', and it would have a direct bearing on the backbone of the trio's next long player (more of which later). It also signalled the band's move away from vocal and *a cappella* based tracks to full-on electric instrumentation. By this time, the family residence was being besieged, not only by the daily chorus of screaming girls over the telephone (which they had grown used to) but also by serious business calls checking out the validity of the brothers as a three-piece combo. The local furore surrounding Hanson was in danger of turning into an uncontrollable whirlwind - a procession of enquiries, questions and general curiosity.

You could almost smell the sweaty, executive fingers deliberating over their pristine chequebooks. Things were most definitely on the up. The track listing for 'MMMBop' is as follows:

01: Day Has Come
02: Thinking Of You
03: Two Tears
04: Stories
05: River
06: Surely As The Sun
07: Something New
08: MMMBop
09: Soldier
10: Pictures
11: Incredible
12: With You In Your Dreams
13: Sometimes
14: Baby You're So Fine
15: MMMBop (long version)

As luck would have it, Christopher Sabec had found favour with Steve Greenberg, Mercury's New York-based Vice President of A&R. Greenberg had been given a tape (which, incidentally, included 'MMMBop') by another Mercury executive, who just happened to be Sabec's girlfriend. Sabec had played her a selection of Hanson tracks, and she had been excited enough to pass them on. After seeing the band's performance for himself at a show in Coffeyville, Kansas, Greenberg swung into action to book them some time at a Los Angeles recording studio. Before long, they had signed a six-album deal, but not before Greenberg had made several special trips to the Hanson family home in Tulsa. His objective was to get to know them better, and on his second visit this was fulfilled when the Hansons took him to an amusement park. Great fun was had by all, yet the most significant factor was the gelling of the friendship between the two parties. Greenberg commented that perhaps it was not the usual type of activity to undertake when courting potential signings, but it worked wonders. The A&R man's only reservation was that he felt the boys needed some kind of mentor, someone to help them make the right kind of record. Steve Lironi was suggested, simply because Greenberg had admired his arrangement of the Black Grape album, 'It's Great When You're Straight...Yeah!', as well as his production work with spooky Liverpudlians, Space. Considering that Lironi was able to keep someone like the wayward Shaun Ryder on the straight and narrow, he was probably the perfect choice to act as a coherent, well-organised foil for Hanson's unquestionable musical capability.

Middle of

A massive overhaul certainly was not needed, as the foundations were already in place. The confidence exuding from the Hanson brothers was seemingly inexhaustible, as they guested on a string of American chat shows. Their own faith in the credibility of what they were doing knew no boundaries, a point illustrated by their appearance on the 'David Letterman Show'. Comments made by the host labeling the trio *"a Partridge Family for the nineties"* and suggesting that *"someone should give these kids their own show"* sparked a cool response from Ike: *"We don't want to be the next Partridge Family. Right now we're focusing on the music."* With this sort of level-headed belief, Hanson are belying their tender years, and winning over the doubters and trivia-mongers as they go. Even executives at Mercury were so electrified by three of the tracks from the 'MMMBop' LP (the title track, 'Thinking Of You' and 'With You In Your Dreams') that they requested the group to re-record them for 'Middle Of Nowhere'. The sessions for the album took place over a period of five months from July to November 1996, and amazingly it was written and recorded during this stint. With Lironi on board as producer, the effort was always going to be made easier, but with Mercury holding their teenage charges in such high esteem, it did not stop there. Justifying the addition of Hanson to the roster by ensuring things worked from the outset also seemed to be another factor in Mercury's logic. The ultra-hip Dust Brothers (who had worked with the Beastie Boys and Sukia and had also arranged Beck's Grammy award-winning 'Odelay') were drafted in to produce two tracks ('MMMBop' and 'Thinking Of You'), while Beck's father (David Campbell) orchestrated the string arrangements. Working with the renowned Dust Brothers (the American equivalent of the Chemical Brothers) gave Hanson the opportunity to spend time at the dandy duo's expansive studio complex. Here they would relax and spend time beside the pool in between rehearsal and recording (at one stage Zac jumped into the swimming pool fully clothed, and ended up bashing his drum-kit while still soaking wet). Ah, the joys of infectious youth. There was no inkling of the boys being overawed by the lofty producers - the sessions were underpinned by a healthy sprinkling of banter and respect between the two parties. When asked to comment, Taylor allegedly retorted: *"I was surprised. They're not really that dusty...."*. But the who's who roster had only just begun to roll.

Nowhere

"We don't want to be the next Partridge Family. Right now we're focusing on the music." Isaac

Other co-writers and collaborators were also called up to flesh out proceedings. These included Barry Mann and Cynthia Weil (who wrote for The Righteous Brothers, The Crystals and The Animals, amongst others). Also Ellen Shipley (Belinda Carlisle's 'Heaven Is A Place On Earth' and 'Circle In The Sand'), Mark Hudson (Aerosmith's 'Livin' On The Edge') and Desmond Child (who had penned songs for many artists, including Aerosmith and Bon Jovi). 'MMMBop' was one of four songs on the album written by Hanson themselves, the others being 'Where's The Love', 'Look At You' and 'With You In Your Dreams'. The latter is probably the most emotionally enchanting song on the record - a gospel-tinged piano ballad inspired by the boys' late grandmother (Jane Nelson Lawyer), and written while she was on the verge of death. Its serene nature obviously sets it apart from the frivolity of most of the other tracks, but what it does highlight once again is the versatility of Hanson's musical prowess. The surprising bonus track (on the CD only, and written by Zac) is 'Man From Milwaukee', which originated from the time when he found himself sitting at the side of the road somewhere in Albuquerque, New Mexico, waiting for his family to repair their broken-down van. In a flash of brilliance he dreamt up a scenario for a song, but as Albuquerque did not sound right, he called it 'Man From Milwaukee' and modified it so it became an ode to aliens!!

Ⓐ ll in all, with its varied mix of styles, it is a hugely competent first commercial outing containing snatches of funky melody, harmony and 1970s soul, with its roots firmly entrenched in the traditional brand of rock and roll. One track ('Speechless') even manages to join the riff from The Beatles' 'Come Together' with a squeaky soul vocal performance, (à la Michael Jackson) and yet it belies the song's sophisticated nature - a story of deceit and betrayal tinged with gothic overtones. Taylor's heart-breaking vocals tend to dominate, but when all three brothers' voices merge together in one fell swoop, (as on 'MMMBop') the moment really is sublime enough to truly recall the heady days of The Jackson Five. It brings together a range of factors - their signature sound swirls energetically through it (wholly reminiscent of the Motown era), but you can also pick out each of their individual contributions easily: Isaac's gleefully loud guitar rhythms; Taylor's keyboard riffs and conga thumping; Zac's sturdy drumming. That 'MMMBop' manages to transcend all international language barriers makes it even more consummate. Released in the U.S. in April 1997, it appeared on the Billboard chart at No.16, climbed to No. 6, and the following week managed to hit the top-spot, selling a massive 500,000 copies. Hanson became one of the youngest ever bands to conquer the American chart. The single's performance in Europe was equally as impressive - No. 1 in six countries, including the U.K. (where it was released on the 26th May 1997). It had already received the accolade of being voted the Radio One Breakfast Show's Record Of The Week, but the following week was even better as the song made it straight on to the station's 'A-list', from which point there was no return. The unashamed pandemonium had kicked in. Amazingly, in America alone, the song had reached an estimated 50 million listeners, after four weeks of heavy airplay following its release. Wading through all this media chaos, it is easy to label 'MMMBop' as a throwaway pop song, yet once you have delved further beneath the glossy exterior, there exists a purposeful theme. In an interview with MTV News earlier this year, Taylor explained the philosophy behind it. *"Really, 'MMMBop' is about friendships. That's what it's about. It's deeper than it sounds."*

*The lads admit they have not met many celebrities to date. However, they have encountered Jewel, Jon Bon Jovi and none other than the Spice Girls. Not bad so far!

Literally, this is well crafted pop that one really should not expect from a band this young. As far as the lyrics go, Hanson stick to perceived clichés or just what they know of the world, wisely leaving all the complicated stuff alone - there will be plenty of time to deal with all that when they are older. The situation needs to be put into stark contrast - the fact is that Hanson have had an almost puritanical childhood. They do not drink, they blush sweetly at the slightest mention of relationships with - God forbid - girls, and their idea of fun involves no more than a trip to an amusement arcade. Yet they have sold enough records around the world to effectively make them millionaires. Even so, they are still in possession of their own developing instincts, giving rise to the odd bout of emotional, pubescent outpouring. The track, 'Madeline', revolves around a broken heart, whilst 'Yearbook Song' centres around the depressing tale of a boy whose photograph did not appear in the high school yearbook. It is a mish-mash of their own experiences to date, combined with the broad picture of their everyday outlook. Real life, if you like. You would have to be a downright cad not to appreciate at least part of it. Mercury's devout faith in the album prompted managing director Howard Berman to make the following statement in support of it:

"I will be genuinely surprised and disappointed if the Hanson album does not turn out to be one of the biggest selling records of 1997. If this is not a platinum album by the end of the year, I think we will have done something very wrong. This is as big a priority as any project can be, but essentially it's a self-generated thing. Hanson made themselves a priority, and the whole company is going with the flow."

Middle of Nowhere

*Taylor enjoys the theatre and anything with a fantasy story including goblins and ghosts.

Track listing for 'Middle Of Nowhere' then, is as follows:

O1: Thinking Of You
O2: MMMBop
O3: Weird
O4: Speechless
O5: Where's The Love

A Minute With You

Having been signed mainly on the strength of the infectious 'MMMBop' track, Mercury's passion for its new protégés is wholly understandable, yet it extends beyond mere verve. A swift leap back to February 1997: the record label has topped up the bill for the filming of the 'MMMBop' video. Shot in Los Angeles with director Tamara Davis (who had previously done sterling work with Sonic Youth, Luscious Jackson and Amp), it certainly did not prove to be cheap. Although it gave the siblings the opportunity to frolic around on the L. A. beaches and indulge in one of their favourite pastimes, rollerblading. Its non-stop cram-as-much-as-you-can-into-five-minutes premise works well as a stage on which the exuberant Hansons can 'goof around', making the most of huge pansies and mock moonscapes to create what can only be described as a 'cartoon circus'. Jump forward to March 1997: Hanson are holed up in an old, dusty Tulsa theatre, again courtesy of Mercury. The purpose is to get them used to playing on a real stage, before they jet off to play an important showcase at the National Association of Recording Merchandisers (NARM) convention in New York City. Session musicians have been hired to flesh out the live sound and Hanson take the opportunity to jam with them, performing with a startling proficiency usually only associated with more seasoned musos. Mercury have hired music director Peter Schwartz to refine their performances, and ensure that as well as being completely ready for action, the boys are totally at ease with their material. Having worked with icons such as David Bowie, Madonna and Toni Braxton, Schwartz is a past master in these matters, and it shows. Although not a task-master, he is nevertheless stringent (in the most affable sense of the word).

The hard work begins to pay off, with a promotional appearance at a shopping mall in Paramus, New Jersey, a benchmark to their growing status, which manages to attract 6,000 exuberant fans. After undergoing a question and answer session, the boys rip into their standard set and perform 'Madeline' and 'MMMBop' (amongst others). Added extras to all this exertion are the relentless television/media appearances for Ike, Taylor and Zac (including MTV and CBS News) - evidence that the sly wheels of publicity are working perfectly as they roar along at a premium blur. Even the British music press have leapt from the bowels of their cautionary stoicism to declare their interest, with prominent features in the New Musical Express, Melody Maker and teen music-bible Smash Hits.

Merely a week into their first UK visit, they were being courted by a vast array of magazines and TV shows, all eager for an exclusive slice of the action. Their success Stateside had pre-empted their visit, and it was apparent that debut single 'MMMBop' would cause quite a stir upon its release here. Hanson-mania had arrived in Britain! The NME's Steven Wells described them as a *"...hot pop songwriting team reminiscent of Bart Simpson, Kurt Cobain and John-Boy Walton craftily infiltrated into the Jackson Five."* Whilst NME colleague Ian Fortnam described 'Middle Of Nowhere' as *"...one of the finest aural experiences to have emerged from mainstream America in the past 20 years."* With that sort of astute praise, Hanson have scant need to fret about decent soundbites - as long as the media circus keeps falling over itself, the juvenile trio can get away with saying very little. It is hard not to envisage the Mercury top dogs looking on, smugly licking their lips and anticipating a substantial return on their lucrative investment. Creep forward again, this time to the 10th of May 1997, and the boys are making an appearance at the Sam Goody record store in Los Angeles to play a brief set. The scene is nothing short of hysteria - mothers are shoving people out of the way so that their daughters have a better view. Teenage girls are yelling hysterically in anticipation of seeing their idols, and people already in the store innocently browsing through the classical CDs have no choice but to leave. According to Mercury's Steve Greenberg, the crushing pandemonium was intense enough to recall the early 1960s when The Beatles were arriving in the States amidst a flurry of interest. *"More than anything, this is like the films I've seen of The Beatles landing at Kennedy Airport, having their famous press conference with the screaming girls everywhere. It's such a precocious comparison to make, but it's the only thing I can think of that reminds me of this."* He continues: *"Everyone told me that kids today would never exhibit hysteria for a young rock band the way they did a generation ago. But kids are kids. They don't change from generation to generation."*

H-O-W-E-V-E-R! There are some corners that are only too eager to twist the Hanson take on life, and use this disparagingly for their own critical purposes. Some of the criticism comes with large slices of humour. For example the web site, where the world of Hanson collides sharply with that of apocalyptic rockers Marilyn Manson (its content centres around Hanson photographs that have been doodled over and defiled to make them look like purveyors of MM's devil-music!).

*When the 'MMMBop' Video was first shown many people thought Taylor was a girl.

Critics are quick to compare them to short-lived acts like New Kids On The Block. They also try to predict that Hanson will go the same way as the two estranged halves of the Osmond family, for whom the pressures of fame finally proved too much during the golden era of the middle-to-late 1970s. Historically, child stars do not tend to have a very long shelf life, but direct comparisons cannot really be made between the Osmonds and the Hansons. Although they produced some fantastic bubblegum pop, the Osmonds were a large family who were prone to bouts of volatile jealousy (infighting occurred because the unknown family members were essentially bitter towards the ones in the public eye). The make-up of personalities and the structured, laid-back attitude of the Hanson clan would suggest that this scenario of family squabbling is unlikely, although one can never accurately predict the future; how well Isaac, Taylor and Zac handle the development from adolescence to adulthood remains to be seen. For the moment, the family Hanson are a close-knit unit - when Hanson have to travel (for whatever reason, be it touring or promotional trips), the whole family follows *en masse* (they all temporarily moved to Los Angeles for the duration of the 'Middle Of Nowhere' sessions). Appreciation exists on all sides - it has been a team effort to get this far and that is obviously the way it is staying. Isaac set the scene in an interview with Kate Thornton of Style magazine at the end of May 1997:

"We want our parents involved because they love us and want what's best for us. Our lives may seem strange to other people, but ask any kid in Tulsa if they would swap playing ball in the park with their friends for travelling the world performing, and what do you think they'd say?"

Taylor reinforces the point:

*Hanson say they intend to be around for years ... no way are they going to be a one hit wonder (good news for us).

"Our parents never pushed us into this - the gigs we played were usually early evening or in the afternoon, so we never really had many late nights."

The sense of realism is what strikes home most about Hanson - they may have been welcomed with a hail of plaudits, but the fact that they could end up on the scrapheap just as quickly has not escaped their notice. When asked what his personal hope for the millennium was, Zac dryly replied: *"I wanna be a worker at Burger King."* And that from an 11-year old, albeit one with a sarcastically swift take on the actualities that could lie in wait around the next corner.

A claim bordering on the ludicrous was also made recently (one assumes in jest) that 'MMMBop' was stolen from En Vogue, who first used it in their song 'My Lovin' (You're Never Gonna Get It)'. It is sung after each rendition of the chorus as a way of leading into the verse - hardly enough to convince the songwriting duo who penned that hit (Denzil Foster and Thomas McElroy) to sue Hanson for infringement of copyright!! It has also been suggested that the band are too chaste for their own time, existing as no more than an adult concept of what teen-pop used to be like during it's 1970s peak. Many vitriolic anti-Hanson sites have sprung up on the Internet of late, but far from being detrimental, they are creating an interesting sub-culture. Debate needs at least two opposites, and Hanson have created a natural forum for the process to occur. A good example of this was to be seen in an article written by Will Hines of Internet magazine Spite. In it, he launches into an attack based on how often 'MMMBop' was played on the radio during the space of a day, using a clever

headline of *'How long must they sing this song?'* Being cynical merely for the sake of it may seem like a fairly senseless pastime, but in this case it elicited an enormous response from its readership. The replies poured in, such as typically sycophantic responses from the pro-Hanson lobby; *"With the world as screwed up as it is, with 'gangsta rappers' glorifying killing cops, and heavy metal rockers talking about suicide, I can't believe you pick on Hanson...you sank pretty low to pick on three all-American boys making it with good music."* Then the inordinately vehement glee of the group's detractors, one of whom described Hanson as *"...ranting delinquents from the romper room."* Some might say that the music they create is outmoded and unfashionable, compared to the street-wise hip-hop chic of many kids today, but that would be missing the point somewhat. The appeal of their music is elastic enough to stretch comfortably across the generation gap, but in terms of the cutting edge of hip-culture it goes even deeper than that. Whole new markets are beginning to open up, linking Hanson to the vogue-elite, and accessing areas in diverse fields such as the fashion industry.

A Minute With You

With
their pale yellow hair and casual
clothing, Hanson betray their apparent innocence with
an androgyny strangely suited to their pubescentia. Caitlin
Moran of The Times is unique in describing Taylor Hanson as the
"...Uma Thurmanesque lead singer...", which (when you consider the
statement for a second) is absolutely spot-on. Dapper schoolboy chic and Hanson
may have arrived in London simultaneously, but they are blissfully unaware of the
impact they are having on each other. Belgium's fashion designer Raf Simons has
based his Autumn/Winter collection on a combined look, covering American
sportswear, street wear from the New York Bronx, the Eton schoolboy ethos and the
well-worn aesthetic of adolescent punk. Backed by a Smashing Pumpkins
soundtrack, Simons' grey flannel school shorts and blazers are modelled on
the catwalks by slim, dainty, Hansonesque dreamboats. These adolescent
boys, plucked from the hipper Antwerp streets, subliminally push
home the message that Hanson hair is not particularly
flattering if you happen to be over twenty.

*Whilst they were in Germany Taylor chipped a front tooth on his microphone and had to be rushed to the dentist. Good news is there was not any serious damage.

Keeping Your Head

The exclusivity of Simons' designs has meant that only a select few London outlets stock his clothes, yet the *tour de force* of the image serves to increase exposure to the Hanson 'look'. Fashion/music journal Dazed & Confused is also a party to this frenzy, committing themselves wholeheartedly to featuring Simons' wares throughout their pages next season. But this is not the first time that teen-popsters have ventured away from music. You may well recall French chanteuse Vanessa Paradis, who had a novelty hit in 1988 with 'Joe Le Taxi' and who has since gone on to become both an actress and a model (for a while she was the visage of Chanel perfume in a series of advertisements). It is unlikely that you will find Hanson endorsing cologne at this stage of their careers, but they have already appeared in advertisements for milk, with said substance adorning their top lips alongside a line which says: *'Where's your moustache?'* Its intention is to promote calcium intake amongst the teenage population, and one is inclined to believe that it will work, especially with the current Hanson-related fervour showing little sign of wavering. They could unwittingly have their thumbs stuck in various pies - new cultural outlets extending them a lifeline where their faces become instant reference points, not just for their looks but also as a reminder or starting point for their music. It is difficult trying to imagine one without the other, but you can bet your bottom dollar on one thing without any hesitation - you will not be getting rid of either for a good while yet.

Fame affects people in strange ways. Some people go completely off the rails while others remain calm and level-headed, and Taylor Hanson would definitely fit quite snugly into the latter category. Only 14, yet with the demeanour of a 20-year old, he is tall and slim and stands out as the real 'looker' of the band. Isaac and Zac have many positive aspects to their character, but Taylor seems to have a charismatic, mysterious edge, and you get the impression that if any one of the trio was going to make a successful solo career out of this at all, then it would be him. The earlier comparison with Uma Thurman may have been top drawer, but his classic features have also brought comparisons with Kurt Cobain and River Phoenix. Add to this the fact that he is a classically trained pianist, and you would think we would have a precocious *enfant terrible* on our hands. Not so. Far from being a brat, he is a down-to-earth, analytical teenager unfazed by the unnatural attention he and his brothers have received. His opinion of how Hanson should be received is remarkably prophetic.

"I don't think of us as having a God-given talent - it's not like we're these child geniuses who woke up one morning, suddenly able to write great songs. We've been snapping our fingers and singing *a cappella* for as long as we've been able."

Always musically and academically gifted, (he has a good knowledge of classic English literature) when he got his first keyboard, true-to-form, he could not stop playing it. He began to learn dance around this time and helped to choreograph some of the early Hanson material, although the dancing phase was abandoned in 1995 in an attempt to concentrate more on their musical ability. Taylor is the one who talks most about the batty antics of Hanson devotees, the one most willing to divulge any fan-related stories, having observed that *"guys want to be friends, and girls do the 'I love you' thing."*

Keeping Your Head

Intriguing, considering that many people mistook him for a girl on first viewing of the 'MMMBop' video!! Indeed, many of the anti-Hanson web-sites focused somewhat predictably on this, singling the middle Hanson out for much of their unnecessary early hostility. Although this was something he originally found more than irksome (possibly due to much ribbing from Isaac and Zac!), this natural frontman has genuinely come to terms with the situation, helped in no uncertain terms by his brothers. The 'all-for-one' philosophy within Hanson is one of their incredible strengths, although it is older bro' Isaac who helps to keep everyone's feet firmly on the ground. Sensible, yet sentimental and calm (and only occasionally prone to the odd nutty outburst), this gentle giant's attitude presumably stems from being part of a big family where everyone has always been willing to share. He has been known to fuss over his hair so much that on one occasion (during a TV appearance) Taylor became so exasperated that he exclaimed: *"Ike, who cares about your hair??!"* Often portrayed as the 'goofy' member of the band, he is in point of fact an excellent all-round sportsman, betraying his so-called clumsy nature. The hobbies go further, with the senior Hanson having a serious attachment to his video camera! It illustrates the sentimental side of him perfectly:

"It looks cool and I love technical things with lots of buttons. I'd be really upset if we lost any of the film because it's full of fond memories. Like the time we caught Tay snoozing at the studio."

When you begin to contemplate that for the past two years he has been engaged in writing a sci-fi novel, you soon understand that we are dealing with eclectic roots here. Then we have Zachary, with whom you could say there was never a dull moment. A budding cartoonist, and profound lover of mathematics (!), some rock critics have christened him 'Keith Moon Junior' (after the original, hell-raising drummer of The Who) but in all probability he is the most technically adept musician of the trio. His elder brothers may playfully taunt him, but this does nothing to put a stop to his impish clowning. If you ignore his well-documented talent of talking and belching simultaneously (!), he is also perceived as being wise beyond his years. Although renowned for being hard to fathom at first, this only lasts until you have got to know him. It is said that the more time you spend with Zac, the more you realise that he is just a cyclone of constant entertainment. Little wonder then that he has also been dubbed the 'young Jim Carrey'.

side from the individual characteristics, there are some things the boys agree on. Current tastes in music, for example. The palate only stretches across modern American bands, (it has been claimed that Hanson have never heard of the Gallagher brothers!). However, they admire a varied collection of artists: Counting Crows, Spin Doctors, Alanis Morrissette, No Doubt, Natalie Merchant (formerly of 10,000 Maniacs) and last, but by no means least, Aerosmith (whose singer, Steven Tyler, they met in April 1997 - an experience Hanson collectively describe as *'their biggest buzz'*. Now, there is a Gallagher-ism if ever I heard one!). Incidentally, Aerosmith's 'Nine Lives' album happens to be a huge Hanson favourite at the present.

*The brothers are all good friends, although they argue sometimes they never really fall out.

Looking Forward

It is now July 1997. 'MMMBop' and 'Middle Of Nowhere' (which globally to date has sold over one million copies) have been stuck in the Billboard Top Twenty since their release, and Hanson have recently been nominated for Best New Artist VH-1/MTV. The release of 'Where's The Love' (the second single from 'Middle Of Nowhere') was eagerly awaited, and having filmed the video in London in June, the band are busy plugging it with appearances at various sites across the United States. The latest series of these at the Meadowlands Fair in Northeast New Jersey - it is only 8 a.m. and teenage daughters are eagerly dragging along sleep-deprived parents. As swarms of them gather, they produce a cacophony of sound which increases once Hanson appear on stage, and it gets even louder once they launch straight into 'Man From Milwaukee'. They are wearing earplugs during these performances, simply because the tremendous noise emanating from the crowd means they cannot hear themselves play! Half an hour later, their standard six-song set is over. Naturally, their armies of fans are ecstatic, but Hanson have even more reason to feel content. Their set is becoming tighter and more confident, to the extent where Ike is improvising with intricate guitar riffs as if his life depended on it. Also, Tay is now at home bashing the keyboards and vehemently swaying backwards and forwards in time to the music, and Zac is just doing his usual thing and being... well, Zac really. Without stopping to draw breath, they are on the bus and off to another location. No respite from the punishing schedule, not while they are booked to play makeshift amphitheatres and converted parking lots in front of seven thousand fans at a time. To say they are enjoying it would be a gross understatement. But what is the reason for the popularity? Why Hanson? Why now? Well, it may have something to do with the huge generation of adolescents world-wide who have come of age, the 10-14 year-old boom that has occurred across the globe. It could also be that the Hansons are providing what the Americans in particular see as good, wholesome entertainment; the trio may be striking a chord with people everywhere, but their evangelical Christian background plays more than a large part in the composition of their uplifting music. The daily itinerary may have 'God's will' printed at the bottom of it, and the sleeve notes inside 'Middle Of Nowhere' may dedicate the record to 'The One', but they appeal to factions of the Christian body purely because their music is so spiritually acute. This has led the American media to labelling them the country's only *'non-dysfunctional family'*, or as one particularly wry commentator described them: *'the anti-Simpsons'*. Whatever is hurled their way, be it snipes or accolades, Hanson just go on doing what they are best at - making irresistible music. They have been lucky enough to get caught up in the middle of a cultural web that is steeped in traditional feel-good factors, where short, sharp hits of the ilk of 'MMMBop' and the Spice Girls' 'Wannabe' are in the ascendancy for the first time since the late 1970s.

Looking Forward

Waiting for the mountains of luggage to come chugging off the airport carousel, they could be just like any other average family on their holiday (save for the burly bodyguards in tow), but that is precisely what makes Hanson so endearing. Walker Hanson, sporting his trademark grey-flecked goatee beard and looking every inch the image of Virgin boss Richard Branson, follows his sons around on their latest mini-tour. Looking out for them and (just like every other father would, given the chance) taking every available opportunity to capture their actions on a video camera that, frankly, never leaves his side. Having left his job to devote his time to the career of his boys, he takes momentous pride in their triumph. Like Ike, his twinkling sentimental streak shows through in his determination to record on film the musical journey of his beaming brood.

It is inevitable that the onset of time will affect the Hanson vision. To an extent, it has already begun - performing on a recent edition of the Jay Leno talk show; the signs were there that Taylor's voice had begun to change. 'Where's The Love' was played at a lower octave than usual due to this, although it did not seem to adversely affect the performance. During the post-song interview, the band was in fine fettle, adopting sarcastic responses to Leno's questions. (Example: *"What's the dumbest question you guys have ever been asked?"* Response: *"How did you all meet?"*) The appearance of the trio has also altered, even since their catapult into the public eye a few months ago. Adorning the cover of American magazine 'Entertainment Weekly' recently, they showed just how much they had grown physically in such a short space of time. The black and white photograph heading the interview (taken by Anja Grabert) is arguably amongst the most flattering, and certainly the coolest of their wide portfolio. Its visual foreshortening represents a picture of crystalline quality, with each brother exhibiting his standard trait. Zac wears wraparound shades, with his hand extended towards the camera in mock indignation; Taylor adopts a sultry pose, staring straight ahead with his arms folded; Isaac has one eyebrow slightly raised, with his lips forming the slightest of smiles. It is the still of a moment in time, but is also saying: "We're ready to move on to whatever may be waiting at the next stage." With dates on prime-time Australian television and an appearance at Canada's colossal Wonderland amusement park preceding the possibility of an Autumn tour, Hanson at least know their plans for the foreseeable future. Beyond that, who can tell?

Assuming Hanson are still around in a couple of years, their voices will almost definitely have completely changed. So may have their philosophies, for that matter. Once they have outgrown their child-star identity, what happens then? Will Hanson still be adored? Or will the pressure of being a rock and roll adult bring the flaxen-haired fairy tale crashing down around their ankles? Well, let us hope not. But you can guarantee that come rain or shine, dewy-eyed Walker Hanson will be in the thick of things with his video camera, filming events for posterity and still glowing proudly at the fact that it is his sons that have climbed up there. Hanson: from the middle of nowhere to the top of the O(a)klahoma tree.

*Isaac says even though most of their songs are about girls, none of them have a girlfriend. He adds that they also sing about aliens. (None of them have an alien either!)

Hanson Quiz

So let us test your Hanson knowledge........ NO CHEATING NOW!

1) Where was the video for 'MMMBop' filmed?

2) Which record label is Hanson signed to?

3) Which member of Hanson damaged a front tooth in Germany?

4) True or False - Hanson have met the Spice Girls.

5) Which cafe played host to one of Hanson's first big gigs?
a) Red Rose Cafe   b) Blue Rose Cafe   c) The Hard Rock Cafe

6) What kind of Mystery weekends does Ike enjoy?

7) How many albums have Hanson released?

8) True or false - Hanson are fans of the Spin Doctors.

9) Name the bands younger siblings

10) What colour leather jackets did Hanson wear during their early shows?

11) What are the boy's star signs?

12) What are Hanson's parents called?

13) How many years have Hanson been performing together?

14) Where was the album 'Middle of Nowhere' recorded?

15) Where will the boys be touring later this year?

answers on page 48

L - R : ZACHARY, TAYLOR & ISAAC

Answers

1) Los Angeles
2) Mercury
3) Taylor
4) True
5) B
6) Murder
7) 3
8) True
9) Jessie, Avie and Mac
10) Black
11) Ike - Scorpio, Tay - Pisces, Zac- Libra
12) Walker and Diana
13) 5 Years
14) Los Angeles - California
15) Australia and the Far East

Scoring

10-15 You are a Hanson nutter and a truly dedicated fan.

5-10 You need to brush up on your handsome Hanson facts.

0-5 Whoops! Go back to the start and read again.